FRANCISCO CALVO SERRALLER

# Velázquez

Fundación Amigos del Museo
del Prado

# Floor plan of the Prado Museum

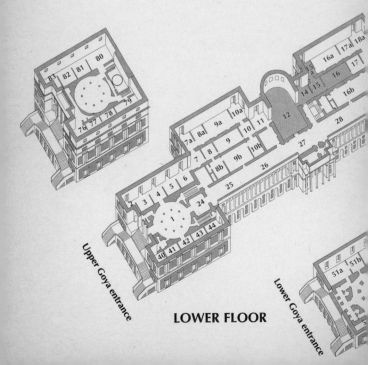

**SECOND FLOOR**

94a

80
83 82 81
79
76 77 78 79

16a 17a 18a
15a 16 17
14 15 16b
12 28
27
7a 8a 9a 10a
7 8 9 10 11
7 8 9b 10b
8b
26
2 3 4 5 6 24 25
1
40 41 42 43 44

51a 51b

Upper Goya entrance

Lower Goya entrance

**LOWER FLOOR**

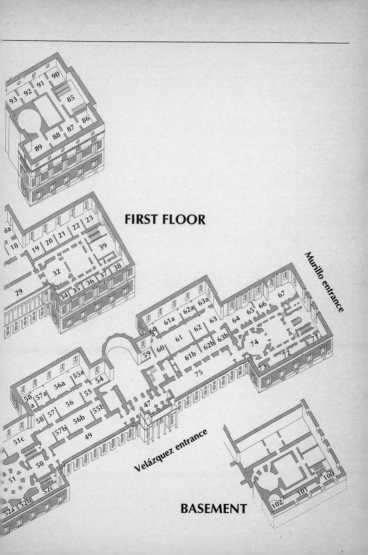

**FIRST FLOOR**

Murillo entrance

Velázquez entrance

**BASEMENT**

Fourth edition: 2001

Cover and interior design by Ángel Uriarte
Translation by Everelt Rice
Axonometric projections by Ana Pazó Espinosa
Edition by Carmen Ponce de León and Manuel Florentín
Layout by Antonio Martín

© Francisco Calvo Serraller
© Fundación Amigos del Museo del Prado
ISBN: 84-922260-5-6
Depósito legal: M. 42.600-2000
Impreso en Varoprinter, S. A. C/ Artesanía, 17. Pol. Ind. Coslada (Madrid)
Printed in Spain

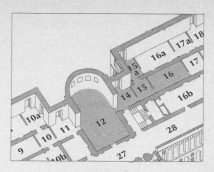

## Introduction

Diego Velázquez was born in 1599 and died in 1660 at the age of 61, which meant a long life in that day and age. It took even longer for him to reach the privileged position universally accorded him today in the history of art. The cause for this delay in critical recognition was due, in the first place, to his isolation in the court of Philip IV, whose service he entered in 1623 and where he remained until his death 37 years later. It was also due to the progressive isolation of his country, which in those moments had already begun its fatal decline. Finally, and above all, it was due to the isolation of his paintings, which were kept behind unbreachable palace walls and which hardly anybody ever saw until the Prado Museum was opened to the public in 1819. But there was no sudden increase, even then, in the appreciation of the exceptional artistic value of his painting. The first generations of visitors to the Prado were still under the influence of Romanticism. Their taste was for the Spanish School, and mainly for its exacerbated naturalism and exalted religiosity, two qualities

5

which were never very characteristic of Velázquez's work.

It was not until the second half of the 19th century and, in particular, from the 1860's to the 1880's, with the development and triumph of French Impressionism that one may speak of any truly international esteem for the Sevillian master. During a trip to Spain in 1865, Manet discovered Velázquez's work and was so impressed that he raised him to the supreme category of 'painter's painter'.

From that time on, Velázquez's artistic destiny was sealed, so to speak, regardless of later fructuations of public taste. No one since then has dared to argue over his place among the best artists of any time or place. Today, Velázquez is to the history of art what Cervantes is to the history of literature: not only the greatest exponent of Spanish artistic genius, but also the most refined and complex prototype of Baroque visual culture and, in general, of the whole modern age.

Velázquez sums up the most outstanding artistic traits of the 17th century. He was endowed with an extraordinary capacity for assimilating the very best of artistic tradition, which he was able to study in detail thanks to the exceptional collection of paintings belonging to the kings of Spain. Even earlier, during his youth in Seville, he had access to the most interesting new developments of the period. A good part of the European painting of the day arrived in Spain by way of this Andalusian city. Later, his trips to Italy allowed him to study these developments even further, and to leave his own unmistakable and highly personal mark as well.

In this sense, almost everyone considers *Las Meninas* to be the most important masterpiece of the 17th century. It was painted towards the end of Velázquez's life and at the height of his artistic maturity. *Las Meninas* hangs in the Prado Museum, along with the majority of his best paintings, since, as we have said, he spent three quarters of his life in the service of Philip IV. In fact, the Prado houses almost fifty paintings that are undeniably his. This is a formidable and unmatchable number given the fact that he was not a very prolific artist, due as much to his phlegmatic disposition as to the energy he spent in carrying out his multiple duties as a courtier. His career at court began in 1623 when he was made Painter to the King and ended with the highly honourable office of Chamberlain of the Royal Palace, having previously served as Usher of the Chamber, Supervisor of Buildings, Gentleman of the Wardrobe, Gentleman of the Bedchamber, and Assistant Superintendent of Royal Works.

But while this dedication to his duties at court often kept him away from his easel, it also provided him with sufficient affluence and the enviable independence to paint however and whenever he pleased. Velázquez was unfettered by the annoying demands of a hypothetical and uncontrollable clientele whose capacity for interfering in an artist's work we should find incomprehensible today. The sense of artistic freedom transmitted in so many of Velázquez's paintings is what we now call 'pure painting', or painting for painting's sake and for no other reason. For Velázquez's day and age this was truly remarkable.

### The Adoration of the Magi
(Cat. No. 1166)

Probably painted for the Chapel of the Jesuit Novitiate College of Seville in 1619. It is Velázquez's first dated canvas. It reflects the tenebrist naturalism that was characteristic of the painter's early Sevillian period. Some specialists claim to recognize various members of Velázquez's own family among the figures: his wife, Juana Pacheco, as the Virgin Mary; his daughter, Francisca, as the Christ Child; his father-in-law, Francisco Pacheco, as King Melchior; and Velázquez himself, kneeling in the foreground, as King Caspar. It is an altarpiece painting, which explains the tightly overlapping figures that are balanced into groups by means of light. This light outlines the figures as if they were wooden sculptures. A remarkable austerity dominates the whole composition, which contains no more sumptuous details than are absolutely necessary, even to the point of exaggerating the poorness of the fabrics. The pleasant charm of the face of the newborn Child, who is completely wrapped in swaddling clothes, contrasts with the pensiveness of the Virgin, a young mother of modest serenity. The twilight landscape in the background adds a bright note of beauty to the composition.

**Christ on the Cross**
(Cat. No. 1167)

This work was painted around 1632 for the Benedictine Convent of San Plácido in Madrid, where it remained until 1808. It entered the Prado 21 years later, in 1829, after a period of vicissitudes. It is the most famous of all of Velázquez's paintings of Christ on the Cross, and undoubtedly one of his best religious compositions. As if quality were not enough, the painting's popularity has partly been prompted by a legend that alludes to Philip IV's forbidden love life and the miraculous doleful tolling of the convent bells that warned of the dangers of such royal misconduct. Legends aside, the painting is a superb Apollonian depiction of the naked body of the dead Christ, whose anatomy is subtly modelled by the light that descends from the upper left corner of the canvas, against a uniformly sombre background in the tenebrist manner of Caravaggio. The serene, classical perfection of the figure is enlivened by the dramatic detail of part of Christ's long hair falling over one half of his face, thus accentuating the shading of the other half. Naturalism and classicism come together here, achieving perfect aesthetic balance and moral depth.

**Coronation of the Virgin**
(Cat. N°. 1168)

Painted for the Oratory of Queen Isabella in the Alcázar of Madrid. Its date is debated, from around 1635 to 1648, although the most likely is the early 1640's. In this solemn and monumental composition, which is based on an inverted triangle, Velázquez has once again achieved a balance between the need for idealization and the verism of the models, whose bearing and beauty (in the case of the Virgin) overwhelm us, but without making the figures seem inhuman or supernatural. From a technical point of view, the virtuosity and variety of the brushstrokes, the rich impasto, and the vivid, luminous colour all make this a prodigious painting. It is also worth noting that scholars have debated the possible iconographical sources of this work, from the Sevillian sculptor Martínez Montañes, or the German artist Dürer, to the Flemish painter Rubens. The canvas entered the Prado in 1819.

**Saint Anthony Abbot
and Saint Paul the Hermit**
(Cat. Nº. 1169)

Painted for a hermitage chapel in the gardens of the Buen Retiro, where the famous palace was built in 1633, the religious subject of this canvas is the legendary visit of St. Anthony Abbot to St. Paul the Hermit, who had preceded him in withdrawing to the solitude of the desert. It was probably painted around 1634. But, as often happens with Velázquez, the extraordinary quality of this painting has prompted many specialists to place it at a later date. The monumental land-scape has Flemish accents that remind us of Patenier and even some of the earlier Venetians such as Bellini. The main subject (the visit) is placed in the foreground. But, in the background, with the anachronistic licence that is natural to painting, we see the later death of St. Paul, with some lions digging an improvised tomb for him, and even further back, other episodes alluding to this pious legend. The raven fly-ing overhead with a piece of bread in its bill is the one that came daily to feed St. Paul. Almost all the details of the landscape are of remarkable strength and quality, and show Velazquez's knowl-edge of classicist Roman landscape painting. The can-vas entered the Prado in 1819.

**The Feast of Bacchus**
(Cat. No. 1170)

Extraordinarily popular, this surprising mythological scene seems more like a laugh 'at' than 'with' the god Bacchus, because of the sarcastic way the subject is treated. A chorus of nine characters of the lowest sort make up the scene, which is considered to be one of Velázquez's first masterpieces. It is certainly the culmination of the period before his trip to Italy in 1629. It must have been painted in the late 1620's, a hypothesis that is established by a document of payment dated 1629. Although it is a composition in the Counter-Reformation manner of 'moralized mythologies', quite akin to the style of Caravaggio and his followers, Velázquez has changed its meaning by the complex device of the many figures involved and by the size of the painting, which is much larger than most genre paintings. There has been much debate as to the iconographical sources, with specialists turning to picaresque literature and carnival celebrations as well as earlier paintings by Titian, El Greco, Rubens, and Caravaggio himself. Velázquez was quite capable of assimilating the work of other geniuses, but he never limlted hImself to 'copying'. In this painting, more than ever, he achieves superb lighting effects and takes the naturalism he learned as a youth in Seville to an extreme. The painting entered the Prado in 1819.

**The Forge of Vulcan**
(Cat. No. 1171)

Everyone agrees on the date of 1630 for this mythological composition, which depicts the moment Apollo bursts into Vulcan's forge to warn him about his wife Venus's unfaithfulness. This means that it must have been painted during Velázquez's first stay in Italy. In reality, the whole composition attests to the Italian lesson: the idealized anatomy of the bodies, the the way the figures are arranged along the picture plane, the wise dramatic involvement of all the characters portrayed, the low-key palette, and the more diffused light which diminishes the naturalist severity of his earlier work. We also find a certain influence from Guido Reni, another naturalist

turned champion of Roman classicism. Finally, it seems that the painting conceals an allegorical intention, which could be to reflect the superiority of art, embodied in Apollo, over mere craftsmanship, a mechanical product of physical labour. This picture entered the Prado in 1819.

**Mars** (Cat. No. 1208)

This painting was inspired by the sculpture called *Il Pensieroso* which Michelangelo made for the Medici Chapel in the New Sacristy of San Lorenzo in Florence. Velázquez's portrayal of the god Mars is satirical, not only for the moralizing reasons of Counter-Reformation origin which produced an earthly vision of mythological gods and heroes, but also of the ever-increasing misfortunes of the Spanish military. Its date is much-debated, but everything seems to indicate that it was painted around 1640. The technique is flowing and the colour, varied. The helmet this naked soldier is wearing is outstanding, as is the armour piled up at his feet. This picture entered the Prado in 1829.

**The Spinners** (Cat. No. 1173)

Considered along with *Las Meninas* to be one of the masterpieces of Velázquez's final period, this mythological scene depicts Minerva's dispute with Arachne over weaving abilities, and the former's punishment of the latter by turning her into a spider. It was probably painted around 1657. The title of *The Spinners*, as it is popularly known, is a later invention and seems to have been inspired by the women who are spinning in the foreground, as if they were workers in the Santa Isabel tapestry factory in Madrid. Even so, Velázquez had used the Baroque recourse of inserting a picture within a picture since he was a young man, and he liked to reverse the order of importance of the story (i.e., putting the trivial forward and the fundamental behind). And this is exactly what he has done here: the background is where we find the key to this painting, by means of the aforementioned mythological story, accompanied by a tapestry with the *Rape of Europe*, by Titian. Not surprisingly, much has been written about the meaning of this painting, which seems to be a declaration of the superiority of art over mere manual dexterity. The picture was damaged in the fire that razed the Alcázar of Madrid in 1734. Even though it was restored at the time, it has come down to us in rather precarious condition, with a later addition to the upper part. It has been in the Prado since 1819.

**Mercury and Argus** (Cat. No. 1175)

This mythological scene depicts the moment in which Mercury, taking advantage of Argus's sleepiness, kills him and rescues the nymph Io, who had been turned into a calf and kept under Argus's watchful care. It is one of a series of four that Velázquez painted for the Hall of Mirrors in the Alcázar of Madrid. Only the present picture has survived, as the other three were destroyed in the devastating fire of 1734. *Mercury and Argus* was apparently painted in 1659 and was thus one of Velázquez's last paintings. It shows the best of his artistic qualities: the gods are humanized and turned into wretched shepherds, but the figure of Argus remains inspired by the Classical sculpture of the *Dying Gaul*. The atmosphere is mysterious and melancholy. The greyish tones, with touches of mauve, are of unparalleled chromatic refinement. The brushstrokes are astonishingly subtle in their lightness. The art of painting seems, here, to breathe freely and easily in the full and independent beauty that is revealed in even the smallest details, such as the scrap of rumpled cloth beneath the sleeping Argus. This canvas entered the Prado in 1819.

### The Surrender of Breda (Cat. No. 1172)

One of Velázquez's most famous compositions, this picture was painted in 1635 for the Hall of Realms in the recently-built Buen Retiro Palace in Madrid. It depicts one of the victorious episodes of the interminable war with the Dutch. In 1625, the governor of the city of Breda, Justin of Nassau, surrendered the fortified town to the general of the Spanish *tercios*, the Genoese Ambrogio Spinola, with whom Velázquez had sailed to Italy a few years before painting this picture. The painting reflects the maturity Velázquez had reached in his art. The treatment of the individual figures in the foreground is brilliant, the light subtly dissolves into atmosphere, and the very free brushwork surprises us in its expressiveness. The theme, which represents the generosity of the victor towards the vanquished, became an exemplary representation which was much imitated later on. The anecdote seems to have been inspired by a comedy by Calderón de la Barca entitled *The Siege of Breda*. But, from an iconographical point of view, as Sánchez Cantón has demonstrated, it comes from an engraving of a Biblical subject by Bernard Salomon. Otherwise, the painting is noteworthy for Velázquez's ability to bring together dramatically a great number of figures in very different attitudes and expressions: some are quite concerned with what is going on, while others seem more distracted. All of them, however, are portrayed with complete naturalness. The painting has been in the Prado since 1819.

**Villa Medici, Grotto-Loggia Façade** (Cat. No. 1211)
**Villa Medici, Pavilion of Cleopatra-Ariadne** (Cat. No. 1210)

These two pictures were traditionally considered to have been painted during Velazquez's first trip to Italy. Today, however, this pair of beautiful and revolutionary landscapes are thought to have been painted during his second trip to Italy, almost twenty years later. Their importance is twofold: they were probably the first landscapes of modern art that were painted, and not just sketched, directly in their nat-

21

ural setting, and they lack a theme, which means valuing painting for its own sake. Furthermore, they are painted with a dramatic sense of light and a freshness of brushwork that is incredibly modern. The bits of architecture and the trees that appear here constructively articulate the deep sense of vivid atmosphere that allows nature to breathe with unusual freedom and spontaneity. Both paintings have been in the Prado since 1819.

## STATE PORTRAITS

**Infante Carlos**
(Cat. No. 1188)

This portrait of Philip III's second son, the Infante Don Carlos (1607-1632), was almost certainly painted around 1626-27, although some say earlier. It is rightly considered to be one of the best portraits that Velázquez painted of the royal family before his first trip to Italy. Less encumbered by the rigidities of protocol that were obligatory in a state portrait of the King, the Infante is depicted with an unsurpassable, natural elegance, based on the spontaneity of the way he is standing as he readies himself for his portrait. The grey emptiness that surrounds the noble figure, and above all, the position of his hands, with the gloved left hand holding his hat while his bare right hand holds the other glove by its fingertips, also form part of this effect of spontaneity, which is so longed for by the dandies of our own times. The Infante's black clothing is a wonder of sumptuousness and nuance.

**Philip IV**
(Cat. No. 1182)

It seems that this portrait is a rerworking or a derivation of the first one Velázquez painted just after he arrived at Court, around 1623 or 1624. Stylistic analysis and radiograph studies reveal quite a few *pentimenti*. This clearly indicates that Velázquez retouched the painting again and again over the years, as was habitual in his case. The king appears dressed in the latest and most sombre fashion, with the *golilla* collar and short cape, as if to set an example after his decree against luxury. It its a typical state portrait in which each element takes on a symbolic function. A certain elegance remains, even though it seems less spontaneous and evocative than the portrait Velázquez did of the Infante Don Carlos at about the same time. The picture has been in the Prado since 1828.

**Philip IV** (Cat. No. 1183)

Painted between 1626 and 1629, this almost half-length portrait of Philip IV was cut down from a larger, unidentified canvas. There is a certain discordance between the face of the very youthful monarch that seems to have been painted in 1625, and the armour and sash adorning the bust which were painted more boldly and flowingly, somewhat in the manner of Rubens. Certainly, Rubens's arrival in Madrid in 1628 produced a very positive artistic shock in Velázquez. The picture has been in the Prado since 1819.

**Infanta Maria,
Queen of Hungary**
(Cat. No. 1187)

This painting was done in Naples in 1630, just before Velázquez returned to Spain after his first trip to Italy. It is a portrait of Philip IV's sister María, and was painted as a keepsake for the King, since the Infanta had become engaged to her cousin Ferdinand, then King of Hungary and later elected Emperor. Velázquez coincided with the Infanta in Naples because that city was one of the stops on her journey to her new kingdom. It seems that this bust-length portrait was a kind of study for a later full-length portrait that was never carried out, though this in no way detracts from its delicacy and charm. The date of its entry into the Prado collection is unknown, although it was probably already there by 1828.

**Philip IV in Armour**
(Cat. No. 1219)

This portrait entered the Prado in 1845 as a work by Velázquez and his assistants. It must have been painted between 1652 and 1654. It forms a pair with the portrait of the same dimensions that Velázquez painted of Mariana of Austria, Philip IV's second wife. There has been much debate as to how much Velázquez contributed to this portrait. More than a few things fall short, though the face and the armour bear the mark of the Sevillian painter's mastery.

27

### Mariana of Austria
(Cat. No. 1191)

Doña Mariana de Austria (1634-1696), daughter of the Emperor Ferdinand III and the Infanta María, Philip IV's sister, was engaged to her cousin, Prince Baltasar Carlos, but after his death, she married her uncle, Philip IV, in 1629. Philip had been a widower since the death of his first wife, Isabella of Bourbon. As Velázquez was in Italy between 1649 and 1651, this portrait must have been done upon his return to Spain, in 1652. Forming a pair with the portrait of Philip IV posing in armour with a lion at his feet, this portrait of the new, young Queen has all of the magnificent painterly qualities that adorned the last decade of the painter's life. Velázquez delights in the sumptuous effects of the dress and the jewels, in the lovely left hand that languidly holds a great white handkerchief, with the red-ribboned bracelets, the elaborate wig, and so forth, all of it executed with enormous freedom, almost without finishing touches. The painting has been in the Prado since 1845.

**Infanta Margarita** (Cat. No. 1192)

Work on this unfinished portrait must have been interrupted in 1659, one year before Velázquez's death. As the story goes, it was continued by his pupil and son-in-law, Juan Bautista Martínez del Mazo, who may have painted the head and the hands of the Infanta, who later became Empress. In any case, the marvellous dress, with its admirable harmonies of pink and silver-grey, is genuinely Velázquez's work. It bears the mark of his startling later manner of painting. The picture has been in the Prado since 1819.

### Las Meninas, or The Family of Philip IV (Cat. No. 1174)

This indisputable masterpiece, not only of Velázquez's career, but of the whole 17th century, was undoubtedly painted in 1656, when the Spanish empire and its prematurely aged monarch were both on the brink of collapse. Wherever the viewer looks, everything in it is enigmatic, from the 'why' to the 'how' to the 'what for' of the composition. A central light falls on the child-Infanta Margarita, attended by two *meninas* (a Portuguese word used at Court for maids-of-honour and pages, which ended up becoming the title of this painting, otherwise traditionally inventoried under the more laconic title of "The Family"). Following the winding line formed by the figures of the Infanta and the maids-of-honour, we come to a female dwarf known as Maribárbola, and to a male dwarf and buffoon named Nicolasito Pertusato, whose foot is resting on, or rather kicking, a sleeping mastiff dog. A bit further back, we see two more members of the retinue: an unidentified *guardadamas,* and Marcela de Ulloa, *guarda menor de damas.* In the background, we see the back-lighted figure of José Nieto, the Queen's chief of tapestry works and later Chamberlain. As he opens the door, we cannot tell whether he is coming or going. Finally, in the image reflected in the mirror hanging on the back wall, we can see the King and Queen themselves. They take the

place of the viewer, and they are either observing the scene or about to enter it. The setting is the artist's spacious and uncluttered atelier. It is a room decorated only with paintings, and kept in a semi-darkness that is broken only by the beam of light that comes from one of the side windows to light up the figure of the protagonist, the

Infanta Margarita, in the foreground. Velázquez sets up a magnificent interplay between the alternating light coming from the side, and the flood of transversal light that crosses the foreground of the scene from front to back and back to front, coming from where we suppose the king and queen to be in the foreground of the room, and from the back, at the door opened by the silhouetted figure of José Nieto. This creates a lively chiaroscuro that reinforces the atmospheric effect of painted air. This blending or overlapping of linear and aerial perspective has long fascinated us as a marvel of representational art. Nevertheless, the painting attracts us more for what it suggests than for what it describes, both in terms of what we would today call virtual reality and from a symbolic point of view. With regard to the latter, it seems that, without detracting from other obvious interpretations concerning the hopeful political fate of the reigning dynasty, the picture is indeed a tribute to the nobility of the art of painting. Rather than rejecting a political interpretation for one that exalts the art of painting, it is possible to see them as complementary, as a mutual complicity and understanding between Philip IV and his favourite painter. Finally, it seems clear that Velázquez has included the spectator in the picture, under the guise of the reflected image of the King and Queen. This explains the prestige of the composition as a reflective representation or, in other words, a reflection on the art of representation. Luca Giordano rightly defined it as "the theology of painting", since the limits between what is painted and what is real are completely flouted here. The picture has been in the Prado since 1819.

**Philip IV**
(Cat. No. 1185)

Probably painted between 1655 and 1660, during the last years of Velázquez's life, this sober, almost half-length portrait of the King is a cruel testimony to a personal collapse that also reflects the collapse of the Spanish monarchy, in turn. It is particularly moving to compare it with the portraits that Velázquez had done of the then-youthful king thirty years earlier. The intimate personal knowledge it reveals and, I would almost dare to say, the identification we discover between the painter and his model, who had lived side by side for forty years, is really quite impressive. The picture entered the Prado in 1827.

## EQUESTRIAN PORTRAITS

### Philip III on Horseback (Cat. No. 1176)

This picture forms part of the series done for the Hall of Realms in the Buen Retiro Palace. It is thought to have been painted in late 1633. Here, Philip III (1578-1621) rides a horse that is rearing against a background landscape. As with the other portraits of this series, except for those of Philip IV and Prince Baltasar Carlos, Velázquez's participation in the execution of the painting seems to have been limited. His role was to oversee and to control the final details of the series. Thus, the horse shows a few touches that are very characteristic of the master, but not many or none at all in the rest of the painting. The picture has been in the Prado since 1819.

**Margarita of Austria on Horseback** (Cat. No. 1175)

Daughter of the Archduke Karl of Austria and Maria of Bavaria, Margarita of Austria (1584-1611) married Philip III in 1599 and thus was Philip IV's mother. Like the others of its kind, this portrait was painted for the Hall of Realms in the Buen Retiro Palace in 1634-35. Also like the rest (Philip III, Philip IV, and Isabella of Bourbon), it is of monumental proportions, although they were all widened along the sides at a later date. We see the queen and her mount in the midst of a landscape, her jewels very much in evidence. Velázquez is believed to have worked only on part of the painting, probably on the beautiful horse, with the rest being done by other hands under his guidance. The picture has been in the Prado since 1819.

## Philip IV on Horseback (Cat. No. 1178)

This painting is cne of the equestrian portraits that Velázquez made for the Hall of Realms in the Buen Retiro Palace of Madrid. Philip IV and his rearing horse are seen in profile and are completely surrounded by a vast landscape, which is particularly remarkable for the beautiful greyish luminosity of its spacious sky. The king is wearing armour with a sash and he carries a baton. His gallant figure is topped off with an elegant plumed hat. The passage of time has revealed several *pentimenti,* such as those in the king's head and chest, and the horse's legs and tail. The painting can be dated around 1635. It entered the Prado in 1819.

**Isabella of Bourbon on Horseback** (Cat. No. 1179)

This is a portrait of Isabella of Bourbon (1602-1644), daughter of Henry IV of France and Marie de' Medici. It was part of the series done for the Hall of Realms in the Buen Retiro Palace of Madrid. Velázquez is thought to have begun it before his first trip to Italy in 1629, leaving it to another painter during his absence. Velázquez reserved the final retouching and corrections for himself, and this went on until 1635-36. This is indicated by the noticeable differences in quality: for example, in the queen's head, and above all the uncovered part of the horse which is of overwhelming quality, whereas the wide skirt is executed with boring minuteness, as someone would do when filling in a form. Neither Philip IV nor his court ever got over the death of this beautiful and cheerful young French queen. The painting entered the Prado in 1819.

### Prince Baltasar Carlos on Horseback
(Cat. No. 1180)

This portrait was painted in 1635-36 to be hung over one of the doors in the Hall of Realms of the Buen Retiro Palace in Madrid. The ill-fated Prince Baltasar Carlos (1629-1646), son of Philip IV and Isabella of Bourbon, was six years old at the time. The picture stands out among the other equestrian portraits of the series for its originality, freshness, and charm of the figure, and for the luminous beauty of the mountainous landscape that surrounds him. The apparently strange perspective, at a very unnatural angle 'from below upwards' was the obvious consequence of the high place where it was to be hung. The painting shows us the truly delightful features of the child rider galloping along with grace and dignity, unhindered by his rich, elegant clothes and general's sash, or the baton he carries so proudly. The picture — in the Prado since 1819 — is exquisitely painted with quick, light brushstrokes. But there is no sign of carelessness, either in the figure or in the marvellous landscape in the background.

## HUNTING PORTRAITS

**Philip IV as Hunter**
(Cat. No. 1184)

This portrait is one of three that Velázquez painted for the 'Torre de la Parada': the King, his brother Ferdinand, and his son Baltasar Carlos. All three are shown full-length, in hunting clothes, bearing arms, accompanied by dogs, and with their figures outlined against background landscapes. This one, of Philip IV, painted between 1634 and 1636, is notable for the *pentimenti* revealed in the left hand, the legs, and the shotgun. The picture has been in the Prado since 1828.

**Cardinal-Infante Ferdinand
as Hunter**
(Cat. No. 1189)

Brother to Philip IV, the Infante Ferdinand (1609-1641) was made Cardinal at the age of 10 and reached historical notoriety mainly as Governor of Flanders, a position he held from 1634 until his death in Brussels. In this picture he is portrayed as a hunter, and, as with all three paintings of the men of the royal family in hunting clothes, it was painted for the hunting lodge called the 'Torre de la Parada', between 1632 and 1636. Against a greyish landscape, and accompanied only by a dog, the Infante is depicted full-length, handsomely dressed, and with noble bearing, while holding a shotgun in his hands and gazing at the viewer, steadfastly but without arrogance or intimidation. This painting has been in the Prado since 1819.

**Prince Baltasar Carlos as Hunter**
(Cat. No. 1186)

This painting can be considered the most beautiful of the portraits of royal hunters that Velázquez did for the 'Torre de la Parada'. There is no doubt as to when it was painted, since the date is inferred by the inscription on the canvas which states that the Prince was six years old at the time. Therefore, it was painted in 1636. Repeating the same formula as the paintings previously described, this one has an even more beautiful and detailed landscape. The figure of the child-Prince has incomparable charm. Velázquez knew how to balance the necessary aplomb of such an important person with the grace and candour of someone his young age. The picture has been in the Prado since 1819.

**Francisco Pacheco (?)**
(Cat. No. 1209)

It is thought that this bust-length portrait of a mature man whose lively face is framed in a full ruff collar could be Francisco Pacheco (1564-1654). Pacheco was Velázquez's master and father-in-law. He was also a respected writer on art, as shown by his treatise *The Art of Painting*, completed in 1638 though published posthumously. Regardless of the identity of the man in the present picture, it is an admirable naturalist portrait that can be dated to around 1619. Velázquez uses effects of light to achieve a perfect depiction of the face while simultaneously reflecting the dynamic spirit of the sitter's inner psychology. The free movements of the model's head have rumpled the folds of the ruff, reinforcing the effect of naturalness the painting produces. It has been in the Prado since 1819.

## Mother Jerónima de la Fuente
(Cat. No. 2873)

While this painting was being restored in 1926, the date 1620 and Velázquez's signature were discovered, making this the first painting we know of that was signed by the artist. It was formerly in the Convent of Santa Isabel la Real, in Toledo, and was purchased from that community for the Prado in 1944. At the feet of the full-length figure there is an inscription that details the nun's merits. The image is painted with surprisingly realistic sever-ity, partly because of the young Velázquez's early naturalist style in which the play of light and dark at times resembles the shadows that fall on carved wooden figures. But it is also due partly to the tight features of the nun herself. Her fierce expression and voluntary stiffness, as if to show her displeasure at having to pose, were not the least bit softened by the painter, who seems to have been uninterested in placing the figure solidly on the floor beneath, thus foreshadowing his later manner of relying solely on shadows to situate upright figures in a suggested space.

### Antonia de Ipeñarrieta with Her Son
(Cat. No. 1196)

No one is sure of the date when this portrait was painted. According to a documented receipt, it was commissioned in 1624. The picture itself may have been painted much later, in the late 1620's or early 1630's. Nor do we know for certain who the child is who appears with Antonia, a lady of Basque lineage who was in the service of Prince Baltasar Carlos. This portrait probably forms a pair with a portrait of Antonia's second husband, Diego del Corral, and shows the full-length figure boxed in vertically by the top and bottom of the picture, an archaistic feature that accentuates the figure's monumental and severe posture.

What stands out most is the lady's face, with her unsettling gaze and deep sobriety broken only by a sensuous, full-lipped mouth. The beauty of her head, placed with magical ligh-tness, contrasts with the stiff geometry of the black dress, which falls rigidly in an old-fashioned manner. This picture was donated to the Prado in 1905.

**Diego del Corral y Arellano**
(Cat. No. 1195)

Like its paired portrait of Antonia de Ipeñarrieta, this portrait of her second husband, Diego del Corral, was also donated to the Prado in 1905. The date of this painting is also debated, between the 1620's and the early 1630's. The vertical, boxed-in composition, the solemn stance of the subject, and the style and fall of his black clothing reproduce the Span-ish prototype of Court por-traiture made popular by Antonio Moro in the times of Philip II. There are, how-ever, two elements that clearly set this portrait apart from those of almost all other Spanish painters until well into the 1630's. On one hand, there is the expressive strength of this high civil ser-vant's serious face; the beauty, complexity, and flu-idity of the black garment; and the general use of colour in the picture. On the other hand is the light that bathes the scene, making the atmos-phere palpable, and hinting at Velázquez's later repre-sentational achievements.

**Juana Pacheco, or
A Sibyl**
(Cat. No. 1197)

This painting was listed in the royal inventories after 1746 as a portrait of Velázquez's wife, Juana Pacheco. There is nothing, however, to prove this traditionally accepted identification. Regardless of who the model is, she is depicted as a sibyl, or as any one of the other mythological characters that have lately been suggested. The picture can be dated around 1632. The figure is shown almost half-length. It is painted with fluidity and is harmoniously inserted into a neutral background with the aid of the yellows of the mantle and the greys of the dress. This picture was added to the Prado after 1828.

**Juan Martínez Montañés** (Cat. No. 1194)

This portrait was painted around 1635-36, when the famous Andalusian sculptor (1558-1649) was in Madrid to model Philip IV's head, the bust of which would later be cast in bronze by the Florentine sculptor Pietro Tacca for the great equestrian figure of the monarch now in Madrid's Plaza de Oriente. A close collaborator of Velázquez's father-in-law Francisco Pacheco, this other great artist was someone Velázquez not only admired but looked upon as almost a member of the family. His attitude is reflected in the portrait, which is profound and penetrating yet retains an element of respectfulness. The picture has been in the Prado since 1819.

### Count-Duke of Olivares on Horseback
(Cat. No. 1181)

Gaspar de Guzmán, Count-Duke of Olivares (1587-1645) was the *valido* or favourite of Philip IV and second only to the King from 1621 to 1643. It was under Olivares's protection that Velázquez began his career at Court in Madrid. Along with Richelieu, Olivares's mortal enemy, the Count-Duke is one of the most interesting and controversial political figures of 17th-century Europe. This equestrian portrait commemorates the Spanish victory over the French at the Battle of Fuenterrabía in 1638, and thus must have been painted at about that time. Velázquez shows the Count-Duke mounted on a horse that is rearing, as if springing into a gallop towards the battle, with the town smoking in the background landscape. Rider and mount are depicted on a diagonal, suggesting depth, which is one of the many Baroque effects of this composition. Its sumptuous theatricality, affected gallantry, and dynamism are quite reminiscent of Rubens. The Count-Duke is seen at his best, at the height of his career, almost on a par with a member of the royal family. This picture came to the Prado in 1819.

**Menippus**
(Cat. No. 1207)
**Aesop**
(Cat. No. 1206)

This pair of imaginary portraits of two famous writers of Classical antiquity, the cynic Menippus and the fabulist Aesop, were painted by Velázquez around 1639 or 1640, apparently to decorate the 'Torre de la Parada'. They both fit into the concept of mocking the legendary heroes of pagan classicism that was quite common in 17th-century Spain. Nevertheless, the moralizing and satIrical nature of both writers is clearly revealed: Aesop, through serious admonition, and Menippus, through caricature. In neither case does Velázquez force the story, except in the naturalistic manner in which he presents them as contemporary beggars. Velázquez's portrayal may, at first glance, produce a misleading impression of monotony; but, on closer observation, thIngs change when greater attention is given to the richly expressive strength of their faces.

**Cristóbal Castañeda y Pernia
('Barbarroja')**
(Cat. No. 1199)

This painting is probably unfinished, and in any case, it has parts that seem to indicate another painter's participation. The attitude and the clothing of Cristóbal Castañeda, who became Philip IV's jester in 1633, recalls the infamous Turkish pirate Khair-ed-Din, nicknamed 'Barbarroja' ('Redbeard'), whose raids caused panic all over the Mediterranean. It seems that the jokes that Castañeda played mocked the ways of braggarts, which he must have felt keenly himself, since, among other things, he was said to "kill bulls". Probably painted in the mid-1630's, this picture shows the jester full-length, with an unsheathed sword, a defiant air, and a harsh and ferocious lock on his face. The image is predominantly sarcastic, and makes little concession to humanity, which is quite surprising in Velázquez, who nevertheless demonstrates the brilliance of his technique in the red costume, though not in the grey mantle that drapes over the buffoon's left shoulder with excessively rigid folds. The picture has been in the Prado since 1827.

**Buffoon called
'Don Juan de Austria'**
(Cat. No. 1200)

The actual date of this painting is much debated, though it was most likely painted between 1632 and 1636. The nickname of this buffoon probably refers to Philip II's illegitimate brother, Don Juan de Austria, who became famous for his naval victory against the Turks at Lepanto. This is perhaps hinted at by the burning ship in the background, as as well as the fancy clothing worn by this grotesque character and the weapons strewn about at his feet, upon a floor of squares done to enhance the effects of perspective, which is admirable in itself. The picture has been in the Prado since 1827.

### Pablo de Valladolid
(Cat. No. 1198)

This buffoon was apparently what was then called an *'hombre de placer'*, dedicated to entertaining the Court, which, as Velázquez has depicted him as if he were about to make a speech, leads us to think of an actor, or at least the caricature of one. We know that his name was Pablo or Pablillos of Valladolid, and that he died in Madrid in late 1648. The picture is thought to have been painted around 1633. It provides the clearest example of the surprising method Velázquez invented in order to eliminate the background, leaving the figure to float in a neutral space and set upon it only by means of the shadows cast by his legs that are spread widely apart. This manner of setting off the silhouette astounded Manet, who incorporated it into his own style. The picture entered the Prado in 1827.

**Francisco Lezcano, called
'El Niño de Vallecas'**
(Cat. No. 1204)

This picture is dated around 1636, though some specialists would have it a little later, towards the early 1640's. The dwarf and mentally retarded buffoon is identified as one Francisco Lezcano, nicknamed 'The Biscayan' because of his Basque origin from Biscay. He entered the service of Prince Baltasar Carlos and outlived the prince by three years, dying in 1649. The figure is traditionally known as *El Niño de Vallecas,* though it has no more real basis or explanation than that of having been called that half a century after his death. The dwarf appears seated on an outcropping of rock in the midst of a landscape. He is dressed in a green hunting suit and holds what seems to be a deck of cards in his hands. The picture is painted with heavy impasto, which denotes the artist's masterful self-assuredness. But it is, beyond a doubt, the dull-witted face, in which psychological precision is once again tied to Velázquez's sense of humanity, that captivates the viewer. The picture has been in the Prado since 1819.

### Jester called 'Calabacillas'
(Cat. No. 1205)

This portrait is perhaps the deepest and most disturbing of the ones Velázquez painted of jesters. Its date has disconcerted the specialists, as well. The quality of Velázquez's style here makes us think it was painted in the mid-1640's, and yet the fact that the jester died in 1639 sets the date back a decade. The face is of a dullard, with crossed eyes and a stupid grin that is repulsive. It becomes even more unsettling insomuch as Velázquez leaves the eyes slightly blurred, using clever psychological tricks that sink into the depths of human existence while neither hiding nor exaggerating the horror. This portrait, furthermore, brings together Velázquez's best painterly virtues, as witnessed in the poor fool's face and hands, but also in the lace of the ruff collar and cuffs, and even the suit itself, with its greenish tones. Two gourds flank 'Calabacillas' ('calabaza' in Spanish means 'gourd'): one large, shiny and golden; the other, dull, humble and closer to what we think a gourd should be. The lighting, which helps complete the suggestion of the space of the floor where the jester seems to be crouching, is also masterful. The painting has been in the Prado since 1819.

**Diego de Açedo, 'El Primo'**
(Cat. No. 1201)

It is not completely certain whether this dwarf was really a jester or not, and if so, whether he had to combine his job with other tasks at Court, such as being in charge of the King's royal stamp. In any case, his small stature and his nickname of 'El Primo' ('The Cousin'), apparently given because of his literary bent, have linked this portrait to the jester series. One reason is the sitter's deformity and the odd setting amid an open-air landscape which is quite inappropriate for a scribe's office, unless there is some surreptitious allegorical intention behind it. But another reason is the deep sense of humanity that Velázquez gives this image. The sombre palette is exquisite; the excellent general effect is undisturbed by the sketchy background landscape. The portrait is thought to have been painted in 1644. It has belonged to the Prado since 1819.

**Sebastián de Morra**
(Cat. No. 1202)

The portrait of this dwarf, who entered Prince Baltasar Carlos's service in 1643 and died in 1649, is dated to between 1643-44. Despite being deformed and a dwarf, his face and his straightforward and penetrating gaze show no hint of mental weakness whatsoever, though they do express a rather melancholy, introspective air. Velázquez delves deeply into the rich facial expression of his model, whose clothing is painted with a great variety and richness of tonalities. The picture has been in the Prado since 1819.

**Head of a Stag**
(Cat. No. 3253)

Donated to the Prado Museum in 1984 by its owner, the Marquess of Casa-Torres, this stag's head must have been painted around 1634, probably along with the series of the royal men in hunting dress. It surprises us for its prodigious realism and the painterly quality it displays.

It is a canvas that has been cut down at both sides and along the top. The verism of this stag's head is the same as that of the dog sitting at Philip IV's feet in the hunting portrait in the Goya Museum in Castres, and owes much to Velázquez's technique of free and open brushwork.

# Other paintings by Velázquez outside the Prado Museum

Velázquez's long and exclusive dedication to Philip IV took up three-quarters of his production. This explains why, of the 120 Velázquez paintings that exist today, almost fifty percent belong to the Prado Museum, whose collection came, first and foremost, from the donation made to that effect by Ferdinand VII. The rest of the paintings have been quite unequally distributed throughout the world, since for the most part they belong to public and private collections in three countries: Austria, the United Kingdom, and the United States of America, or to be more exact, in only three cities: Vienna, London, and New York.

In Vienna, the former capital of the Austro-Hungarian Empire and home of the Habsburg dynasty, there are paintings of this family, such as the portraits of *Philip IV* and *Isabella of Bourbon,* both from 1632; those of *Prince Baltasar Carlos,* from around 1640, and the *Infanta María Teresa* (c. 1652); three of the child *Infanta Margarita,* thought to have been painted successively in 1654-55, 1656, and 1659; and one of *Prince Philip Prosper* (1659).

In the cases of London and New York, beyond any dynastic considerations, there was a vigorous kind of collecting that predominated from the beginning of the 19th century. And, we must not forget the presence of the British in Spain during the Peninsular War. In any case, in London we find works of such importance as *St. John on the Isle of Patmos* (1618), the *Immaculate Conception* (c. 1618), *Christ in the House of Martha and Mary* (1619-1620), *Philip IV in Brown and Silver* (1635), *Philip IV Hunting Wild Boar* (1638?), *The Toilet of Venus* (1650?) and *Philip IV* (1655-59?), all belonging to the National Gallery. London is also where the Wallace Collection owns two very relevant pictures: a portrait of *Prince Baltasar Carlos at the Age of 3* (1632) and the *Lady with a Fan* (c. 1646). Also in London, the Wellington Museum can be proud of owning *Two Young Men at Table* (1618?), *The Waterseller of Seville* (c. 1620) and *Portrait of a Bearded Man* (1632-34).

In New York, there are three institutions that house such treasures, starting with the Metropolitan Museum's *Supper at Emmaus* (c. 1620), *Philip IV* (1624), *Juan de Pareja* (1650), and the two portraits of the Infanta María Teresa, dated around 1651 and 1652-53, repspectively. The Hispanic Society of this city owns a portrait of the *Count-Duke of Olivares* (1625?), *Young Girl* (1624?) and *Cardinal Camillo Astalli Pamphili* (1650). The Frick Collection owns the *Philip IV at Fraga* (1644). Finally, other museums of the world that stand out because of their Velázquez paintings are the National Gallery in Washington (*Woman Doing Needlework* (1640?); the Boston Museum of Fine Arts (*Luis de Góngora* (1622) and *Prince Baltasar Carlos and a Dwarf* (1631); the Cleveland Museum of Art (*The Buffoon Juan de Calabazas,* 1626?); the Art Institute of Chicago (*St. John the Baptist in the Desert,* 1620?); the Staatliche Museen of Berlin (*Three Musicians,* 1618? and *Portrait of a Lady,* c. 1632); the Gemaldegalerie of Dresden (*St. Matthew,* c. 1619, *Juan Mateos,* c. 1632, and *A Knight of the Order of Santiago,* c. 1645); the National Gallery of Scotland, in Edinburgh (*Old Woman Cooking Eggs,* 1618); the Hermitage, in St. Petersburg (*Young Man,* c. 1620, *Three Men at Table,* c. 1620, and the *Count-Duke of Olivares,* c. 1635); the Doria Pamphili Gallery in Rome (*Pope Innocent X,* 1650); the Musée des Beaux-Arts of Rouen (*Democritus,* 1625-40); the National Gallery of Ireland in Dublin (*Supper at Emmaus,* c. 1617-18) and others.

Other collections in Spain, aside from the Prado, are logically and comparatively plentiful. We shall limit ourselves to pointing out that it is necessary to visit El Escorial to see *Joseph's Bloodied Coat Brought to Jacob* (1630); The Archbishop's Palace in Seville (*St. Ildefonsus Receiving the Chasuble,* c. 1623); and Orihuela, where the Diocesan Museum of Sacred Art houses *The Temptation of St. Thomas Aquinas* (1631?).

## Basic Chronology

**1599:** Birth of Diego Rodríguez de Silva y Velázquez in Seville on 6 June.

**1609:** Apprenticed in the studio of Francisco Herrera the Elder.

**1610:** Changes to studio of Francisco Pacheco, where he will complete his studies.

**1617:** Authorized as independent master and sets up his own studio in Seville.

**1618:** Marries Juana, daughter of his master, Pacheco.

**1619:** Birth of Velázquez's first child, Francisca, future wife of the painter Martínez del Mazo.

**1622:** First trip to Madrid.

**1623:** Second trip to Madrid, where he settles permanently on being named First Painter to Philip IV.

**1627:** Appointed Usher of the Chamber.

**1629:** Sails for Italy, where he remains a year and a half.

**1633:** Appointed Supervisor of Buildings.

**1634:** Appointed Gentleman of the Wardrobe.

**1635:** Finishes *The Surrender of Breda* for the Hall of Realms of the new Buen Retiro Palace.

**1643:** Accompanies the King, on military campaign in Aragon. Appointed Gentleman of the Bedchamber and Assistant Superintendent of Royal Works.

**1649:** Second trip to Italy, to buy old and new works of art.

**1651:** Returns to Spain after a happy and lengthy stay in Italy, where he was admitted as Member of the Academies of St. Luke and the Virtuosi of the Pantheon.

**1652:** Appointed Chief Chamberlain.

**1656:** Paints *Las Meninas* and oversees the installation of paintings in El Escorial.

**1658:** Finally admitted to the Order of the Knights of Santiago after many annoying attempts.

**1660:** As Chief Chamberlain he attends the ceremonies of the Peace of the Pyrenees with France on the Isle of Pheasants in the Bidasoa River. On returning to Madrid, he falls ill and dies on 6 August, at 3:00 p.m. A few days later, his widow Juana Pacheco dies. He is buried in the parish church of San Juan Bautista.

# Basic Bibliography

ALCALÁ-ZAMORA, J. N. (Ed.): *La vida cotidiana en la España de Velázquez,* Madrid, 1989.

ALCOLEA, Santiago: *Velázquez,* Barcelona, 1989.

ANGULO IÑIGUEZ, D.: *Vélazquez. Cómo compuso sus principales cuadros,* Madrid, 1947.

BARDI, P. M.: *La obra pictórica completa de Velázquez,* Barcelona, 1982.

BATICLE, J.: *Velázquez. Pintor hidalgo,* Madrid. 1990.

BERUETE, A. de: *Velázquez,* Madrid, 1987.

BROWN, J.: *Velázquez. Painter and Courtier,* New Haven-London, 1986.

BROWN, J. and ELLIOTT, J. H.: *A Palace for a King. The Buen Retiro and t Court of Philip IV.* New Haven-London, 1986.

BLENDÍA, R. and ÁVILA, A.: *Velázquez,* Madrid, 1987.

CALVO SERRALLER, F.: *Velázquez,* Barcelona, 1991.

—: *Las Meninas de Velázquez,* Madrid, 1995.

CAMÓN AZNAR, J.: *Velázquez,* 2 vols., Madrid, 1964.

Catalogue of the *Velázquez Exhibition,* Metropolitan Museum, New York, 1989.

Cruzada Villaamil, G.: *Anales de la vida y de las obras de Diego Silva Velázquez,* Madrid, 1885.

DÍEZ DEL CORRAL, L.: *Velázquez, la monarquía e Italia,* Madrid, 1979.

GÁLLEGO, J.: *Velázquez en Sevilla,* Seville, 1974.

—: *Diego Velázquez,* Barcelona, 1983.

—: *Velázquez,* Madrid, 1994.

GARRIDO PÉREZ, C.: *Velázquez, técnica y evolución,* Madrid, 1992.

GAYA NUÑO, J. A.: *Bibliografía crítica y antológica de Velázquez,* Madrid, 1963.

—: *Velázquez,* Barcelona, 1984.

GUDIOL, J.: *Velázquez, 1599-1660,* Barcelona, 1973.

HARRIS, E.: *Velázquez,* Oxford, Phaidon, 1982.

JUSTI, C.: *Velázquez y su siglo,* Sp. edition, Madrid, 1953.

LAFUENTE FERRARI, E.: *Velázquez,* Edición completa, Barcelona, 1944.

—: *Velázquez. Estudio bibliográfico y crítico,* Barcelona, 1966.

LÓPEZ-REY, J.: *Velázquez: The Artist as a Maker. With a Catalogue Raisonné of his extant Works,* Lausanne-Paris, 1981.

MCKIM-SMITH, G. y NEWMAN, R.: *Ciencia e historia del arte: Velázquez en el Museo del Prado,* Madrid, 1993.

MARAVALL, J. A.: *Velázquez y el espíritu de la modernidad,* Madrid, 1960.

MARÍAS, F.: *Diego Velázquez,* Madrid, 1995.

—: *Otras Meninas,* Madrid, 1995.

MOFFITT, J. F.: *Velázquez, práctica e idea: estudios dispersos,* Málaga, 1991.

MORÁN TURINA, M.: *Velázquez,* Madrid, 1993.

ORTEGA Y GASSET, J.: *Velázquez,* Madrid, 1959.

PANTORBA, B. de: *La vida y la obra de Velázquez,* Madrid, 1955.

VV.AA.: *Varia velazqueña,* 2 vols., Madrid, 1960.

—: *Velázquez y lo velazqueño,* Madrid, 1961.

—: *Velázquez y el arte de su tiempo,* Madrid, 1991.

—: *Reflexiones sobre Velázquez,* Madrid, 1992.

# General Information on the Prado Museum

## EDIFICIO VILLANUEVA
Paseo del Prado, s/n
28014 Madrid
*Telephone:*
91 330.28.00
*Fax:*
91 330.28.56
*Information:*
91 330.29.00
Wheelchair access available

## VISITING HOURS
*Tuesday through Saturday:*
9:00 a.m. to 7:00 p.m.
*Sundays and holidays:*
9:00 a.m. to 2:00 p.m.
Closed on *Mondays*

## ENTRANCE FEES
General Admission      *500 ptas*

Spanish youth card, student
card, or international equiva-
lents.
Cultural and education group
rates (by advance request)
91 330.28.25)      *250 ptas*

Senior citizens over 65 or
pensioners.
Members of the Fundación
Amigos del Museo del Prado.
Cultural and educational vol-
unteers      *Free*

## Free General Admission Days
*Saturdays*, from 2:30 p.m. to
7:00 p.m.
*Sundays,* from 9:00 a.m. to
2:00 p.m.

## *Coffee Shop*
*Tuesday to Saturday:*
9:30 a.m. to 6:30 p.m
*Sundays and holidays:*
9:30 a.m. to 1:30 p.m.

## *Restaurant*
*Monday to Saturday:*
9:30 a.m. to 6:30 p.m.

## *Shops*
*Tuesday to Saturday:*
9:30 a.m. to 6:30 p.m.
*Sundays and holidays:*
9:30 a.m. to 1:30 p.m.

## HOW TO GET THERE
*Metro:*
Atocha, Banco and Retiro
stations

*Bus:*
Numbers 9, 10, 14, 19, 27,
34, 37, 45

*From the airport:*
Airport shuttle bus to Plaza de
Colón, then No. 27 bus

## General Information about the Fundación Amigos del Museo del Prado
Museo del Prado
c/ Ruiz de Alarcón,nº 21 –
bajo. 28014 Madrid
Tel: 91 420.20.46
Fax.: 91 429.50.20
E-mail: famprado@canaldata.es

*Office hours:*
Monday to Friday, from 9:30 a.m.
to 2:30 p.m.